Irina Vysotskaya

International News: Specifics of Comprehension and Editing

AF513736

Irina Vysotskaya

International News: Specifics of Comprehension and Editing

On the example of Reuters

ScienciaScripts

Imprint
Any brand names and product names mentioned in this book are subject to trademark, brand or patent protection and are trademarks or registered trademarks of their respective holders. The use of brand names, product names, common names, trade names, product descriptions etc. even without a particular marking in this work is in no way to be construed to mean that such names may be regarded as unrestricted in respect of trademark and brand protection legislation and could thus be used by anyone.

Cover image: www.ingimage.com

This book is a translation from the original published under ISBN 978-620-2-09599-0.

Publisher:
Sciencia Scripts
is a trademark of
Dodo Books Indian Ocean Ltd. and OmniScriptum S.R.L publishing group

120 High Road, East Finchley, London, N2 9ED, United Kingdom
Str. Armeneasca 28/1, office 1, Chisinau MD-2012, Republic of Moldova, Europe
Printed at: see last page
ISBN: 978-620-7-99299-7

Copyright © Irina Vysotskaya
Copyright © 2024 Dodo Books Indian Ocean Ltd. and OmniScriptum S.R.L publishing group

Table of contents

Introduction

Information agencies are specialized information enterprises (organizations, services, centers) serving mass media. Their main function is to provide operative political, economic, social, cultural information to editorial boards of newspapers, magazines, television, radio broadcasting, as well as to other institutions, organizations and individuals. Functioning is focused on news gathering.

The birth of Reuters traces the historical milestones of all major news agencies. Companies that started with the dissemination of news, with the development of information technology, have evolved into specialized centers for a particular line of business (e.g., financial sphere, trade relations).

The role of information journalism is currently growing considerably. After all, the amount of information coming to a person is so great that he or she is no longer able to sort through it independently, determine the criteria of truth and make the right decision.

In the pre-industrial environment, the main information load consisted of personal contact with another person. Later, book culture was formed, where printed media of mass communication prevailed. In post-industrial society, screen culture, created on the basis of audiovisual technology, has become increasingly important. From now on, the production, storage, transmission and consumption of information is based on a fundamentally different technological basis.

This paper is devoted to the study of the history of the development of the Reuters news agency and the study of the specifics of news comprehension and editing. To date, the Reuters news agency is the largest corporate organization, which is engaged in the search, accumulation and dissemination of information. Increased interest in the novelty of messages is associated with the effective and purposeful use of accurate, timely information to solve the problems of dynamic development of the public, which, in turn, is a condition for sustainable development of humanity in the modern world. Information requires a serious attitude to itself, because it is the intellectual property of the country and its citizens, a resource of society. Therefore, the relevance of the topic is indisputable.

Today, there are a very large number of information agencies operating at both national and transnational levels. "Reuters is one of the leading providers of economic information to financial market participants.

The purpose of the work is to identify and study a set of methods and tools used by the world news agency "Reuters".

Historical aspect of Reuters' development

The British news agency Reuters is one of the largest news agencies in the world. It covers a very wide range of services for collecting, creating, providing and processing information. Such innovations as the first electronic information products and the first electronic transactions were an important factor in the rapid development of global financial markets. The agency is engaged in the production and transmission of information materials for various media. The main activity, which generates 90% of the corporation's income, is to provide market professionals with important market information, analytics and reports on commodity and financial markets. In addition, it produces electronic news graphics and provides telecommunications services.

Reuters came into being through the efforts of Julius Reuter. He became famous for his entrepreneurial activity in the field of news gathering. After all, in the middle of the XIX century, news reports appeared on the pages of publications more often than other genres of journalism, so they turned into a very profitable commodity. In this regard, Reuter chose news as the object of his attention because in his time the market had a greater need for information than ever before. On the one hand, there was a growing public demand for news, and on the other hand, technology was developing rapidly to meet this need.

Julius Reuter was born in 1816 in the middle German city of Kassel to an educated and respected Jewish family. In the 30's in Göttingen, a university town, Julius attended lectures of Carl Friedrich Gauss, the founder of modern mathematics. The scientist conducted the first experiments on the transmission of an electrical signal through a wire. Gauss had little interest in the practical application of the discovery in magnetism, but Reuter realized at this time that these discoveries would revolutionize communication, and mankind would soon be able to communicate by telegraph over any distance. This discovery later prompted the formation of the world's largest telegraph agency.

In 1848, Julius Reuter begins working at the Gavas agency. Among the most important acquaintances are the colleagues of the young specialist: Sigismund Engländer and Bernard Wolf. Thus, within a year, the founders of three future major news agencies worked under the same roof. However, Reuter's desire to become his own boss increased every year. To realize his goal in early 1849, he began to publish his own newspaper in Paris, taking advantage of the lack of tax on printing. His first office was a small room on the top floor of one of the houses on the street of the French Enlightenment philosopher Jean-Jacques Rousseau. The newspaper was news of various kinds, from gossip, to secular information, to reports on the meeting of the National Assembly, to prices on the Paris Stock Exchange. The editor was Reuter. The translation work (from French to German) was done by his wife. The newspaper was then sent to Germany. Soon the income did not exceed the expenses. This led to the printing equipment being seized by creditors. However, this fact did not make Reuter give up his dream. After moving to Germany, he opened the "Telegraphic Relief Office".

The German city of Aachen in the mid-19th becomes key in the transmission of news and the most important communication point between Belgium, the Netherlands and Germany. V.V. Voroshilov writes that "there were certain prerequisites for opening an office here: 1. political - relaxation of control over information flows, 2. technological - widespread use of the telegraph line" [7, p. 15]. But even here Reuter encountered difficulties. After the French government opened the telegraph line "Paris - Brussels" from Aachen to Brussels there was a gap of 90 kilometers. Thus, the traditional transmission of messages by rail was replaced by pigeon mail. Reuter was the first person to put this type of information delivery on a regular basis. This is how the basis for the establishment of a news agency was formed. The first major newspapers to subscribe to the services of the "Office for Assistance in the Transmission of Telegraphic Messages" were the "Kölnische Zeitung" and the "Independence Belge". Attempts to become the main intermediary between England and the rest of Europe proved impossible, so in the summer of 1851 Reuter and his wife returned to London.

According to M.I. Skulenko, "in the middle of the XIX century London was a rapidly developing economic center" [34, p. 23]. [34, c. 23]. The economic basis of England's success at that time was considered the freedom of trade. After the abolition of stamp duty on newspapers, the readership and circulation of publications increased. The emergence of news agencies was influenced by the following factors in the development of the British press: 1) the increase of state control and the development of print pluralism; 2) the transformation of the press into a business tool; 3) the decline of interest in the party press; 4) the finalization of the journalistic profession.

Julius Reuter's Underwater Telegraph Company was founded on October 4, 1851. This date is considered to be the opening day of the Reuters news agency. By this time, the founder had considerable capital to start the business and had numerous contacts in the main European centers. The office of the new company was located near the London Stock Exchange. Twice a day Reuter supplied London brokers and traders with stock information by telegraph line. Also, business people in major European cities such as Hamburg, Antwerp, Trieste, Odessa, and Gdansk were subscribers. In 1853, the Underwater Telegraph Company was given a new name: the Continental Telegraph Company.

For several years, Reuter failed to make a breakthrough in delivering news to newspapers. The Times was considered a major English newspaper, with correspondents in various parts of the globe - the United States, China, India and the Middle East. The editor-in-chief, Morris, was reluctant to establish contact with the Underwater Telegraph. The turning point of this policy was 1858. At this time, the Morning Advertiser and the Daily Telegraph began publishing Reuter's reports. Morris in the deal with Julius found a favorable moment - the agreement will cut costs in half. Thus, the Times became a partner with the Continental Telegraph. Only the editors of the newspaper at every opportunity tried to show that the correspondents work with no less efficiency.

Reuter's credibility was increased by the publication in the Times of January 10, 1859, of a dispatch signed "Continental Telegraph," which reported an important speech by the King of Sardinia at the opening of his state's parliament. An even greater success was reported on February 7 of the same year, when the text of a very important speech of Napoleon the Third before the chambers of the French National Assembly was obtained by Reuter's agents before it was delivered. V.V. Voroshilov notes: "In this speech Napoleon said: "I hope that our peace with Austria 'will not be hindered by anything.'" In the diplomatic language of the time it actually meant that the war is close" [7, c. 302]. The significance of the publication allowed us to talk about the news agency as a completely new form of news reporting.

The audience of the Continental Telegraph was mostly middle-class men of liberal views. They valued accuracy in the presentation of information, so the office needed to maintain prestige. During France's short but bloody war against Austria in 1859, Reuter placed a correspondent on both front lines. This ensured both the reliability of information and the efficiency of collection. The company was the first to report on the decisive battle of Solferino, and the next day relayed information from the camp of the defeated in Vienna.

Such tactics and technologies emphasize the high level of the agency's development at the time. This is evidenced by the fact that it was Reuters that was in high demand in the British press. In 1865, the company was reconstructed, firmly establishing the name "Reuters". The goal was to find economic solutions to raise additional funds to develop the agency to create a wide network of messages. In 1878, Julius Reuter resigned as managing director and handed over authority to his son, Baron Herbert de Reuter. The main merit of the new owner was to raise the philological level of information presentation. In addition, he managed to strengthen the reputation of Reuters as an objective agency.

Reuters' activities during the World Wars

The leadership of Baron Herbert de Reuter is associated with the creation of some adventurous projects. The first of them concerned the creation of an advertising service. However, management errors and the general decline of trade in Europe did not allow to increase the financial component of the company. The second idea was the creation of the "Reuters Bank". However, the unreliable foundation of the bank and blatant speculative nature of its operations predetermined its further existence.

During World War I Reuters financial situation required investment. The company was in need of reconstruction. In 1915, Roderick Jones was appointed as general manager. In order to get the company out of the crisis, it was necessary to be elected from the shareholders. The problem was that their number was too large. Jones, together with the company's chairman Mark Napier, bought back the shares. Reuters became a private enterprise again. Also, it was necessary to reconstruct the bank, as it was on the verge of bankruptcy. The buyer was the well-known financial speculator Clarence Heytree.

In the 1920s, Reuters needed austerity in order to stabilize financially. Consequently, a 10% cut in staff salaries was made. Meanwhile, in 1925, a report submitted by the financial department to the company's management contained the following statistics: revenues from the news bureau were not growing, profits from advertising activities were insignificant, and the telegraph and transmission service, which had been the pride of the agency for many years, had become unprofitable. The only way out that the company's management could offer was to sell at least part of the stock. Gradually, the choice was made in favor of the option of co-ownership of Reuters by the Press Association. The conclusion of the agreement meant that Reuters effectively gave up control of the agency to the British press.

However, the 1930s were marked by a new financial crisis. The number of words in stories was cut by a quarter. Working in uncomfortable conditions led to more frequent mistakes by correspondents, which affected the reputation of the company as a whole.

There were even mistakes in reports of national importance. For example, false information about the secret negotiations that the French Foreign Ministry had with Mussolini's government in 1937. As a result, Roderick Jones turned to the British government for help. Prime Minister Chamberlain Jones' condition was that Jones nominate government representatives for key positions at Reuters. However, Jones during his reign adhered to the policy of maintaining the independence of the agency from the government. The situation required urgent action. As a result, Roderick decided to sign a secret agreement with the government on financial cooperation in 1938. Under the agreement, without the knowledge of the Reuters Board of Directors, the British government would pay the agency 18,000 pounds francs a year in exchange for its influence over the agency. In addition, Roderick would relinquish some of his powers and eventually cease to be active altogether.

Soon some details became clearer for the Reuters Board of Directors and the Reuters-Government agreement was opened. S.I. Smetanina draws attention to the fact that "in 1941 Roderick Jones announced his resignation. In a letter to the Times, he noted: "I could have allowed the agency with its solid capital and excellent reputation to go to public sale. But a free market and a public sale of shares would expose Reuters to the threat of unwanted influence, and possibly control." Three years later he explained to Michael Ewing, the owner of the Glasco Herald, that he was "too tired and exhausted by the ominous events of recent years that any thought other than resignation disgusted him" [35, p. 35] [35, c. 35]. Nevertheless, it should be noted that his company stayed afloat during the years of the global financial crisis.

The new chairman of Reuters, Samuel Story, emphasized the need to strengthen Reuters' independence and efficiency in the face of increasing competition from U.S. agencies. The possibility of distributing shares not only to the Press Association but also to the Newspaper Owners Association was considered. In addition, the idea of a possible trust agreement between Reuters shareholders was suggested. The purpose was to warn the agency against outside interference and influence, primarily from the British government. Also, such a plan would protect the company from internal corruption and violations of work standards by directors or managers.

At the board meeting there was a discussion about buying shares. Ewing remarked that selling half of Reuters' shares would give Britain a stronger and more influential news agency. It would also increase the value of the shares themselves. The main argument for rejecting the sale plan was that the members of the proposed trust would have no power. In the end the trust resolution was defeated by 43 votes to 17, but the stubborn opposition of Samuel Storey allowed an attempt to be made to accomplish its purpose. At the meeting, some Labour MPs expressed fears about whether the Reuters transformation would entail existing independence. M. Tangate recalls that "the British Information Minister Brandon Breyken said that all changes are under strict government supervision: "Reuters is not Canterbury Cathedral, but a business enterprise, so it is necessary to take steps to improve the efficiency of its work" [37, p. 68] [37, c. 68]. After this speech, the debate subsided. No resolution was adopted.

The Newspaper Owners Association expressed skepticism about the possibility of a trust agreement. The preamble to the 1941 agreement stated that "the execution of a trust deed is in the national wartime interest. The Press Association and the Newspaper Proprietors Association, recognizing that the present emergency and the uncertainty of the future require special precautions to safeguard the national interest, then Reuters should be organized in such a way as to maintain its status as the world's leading news agency under all circumstances." According to M. Tangate, "the Press Association and the Newspaper Owners Association hereby confirm their mutual agreement that they will consider their holdings in Reuters as part of a trust agreement, not as an investment" [37, p. 69] [37, c. 69]. In addition, goals were set so that: 1) Reuters would never fall into the hands of any group or faction; 2) the integrity, independence, and freedom of the agency would always be preserved; 3) the company would be managed so that it would supply unbiased and reliable news to newspapers in the British Dominion and other foreign newspapers, and to agencies with which it would be bound by contracts; 4) the company would give credit to the interests it would serve apart from those of the press; and 5) every effort would be made to maintain Reuters' status as a leading news agency." The trust was to operate for a minimum of 21 years.

At a time of fierce debate over the future of Reuters, the headquarters was under threat. At the height of World War II, during the bombing of London, a bomb hung from trolleybus wires right under the windows of the agency's building. It is worth noting that it was the coverage of World War II events that allowed Reuters to demonstrate the high professionalism of its correspondents and establish itself as a global agency after the collapse of the British Empire.

At the beginning of the war, the agency had no correspondents on the battlefields. Soon Reuters organized a system of information gathering by radio and competed with the Americans due to the quality work of the "listening service". The first successful correspondent of "Reuters" in the war years can be called Desmond Tye. In April 1940, this man was in Oslo at the time when the Germans entered it, but managed to leave for Sweden, having previously reported on the occupation. Miraculously he got past the German pickets. He became a correspondent for the agency and, being in Paris when the Germans were advancing, barely made it to England. He then covered events in Egypt in 1941, in 1943 the Allied takeover of Italy. He was the first to give information about the landing at Salerno. Serious successes were achieved by Reuters in covering the war between Germany and the Soviet Union. On June 21, 1941, the German's promise of a "quiet weekend" alerted correspondents. Shortly after midnight came a report of Hitler's criticism of the Soviet Union. Risking its name, Reuters published a report of a German attack on the Soviet Union. The event turned out to have been foreseen. In the summer of 1942, the agency sent correspondent Harold King to the Soviet Union. He sent war reports to London in Russian. V.V. Voroshilov recalls King's messages in his memoirs: "During the years of his work in Russia, messages under his signature were published in thousands of newspapers" [7, c. 322]. In 1943, King personally received a message from Stalin about the dissolution of the Comintern. This action on the part of the government of the Soviet Union was insisted on by Western countries.

That same year, Reuters was the first to report the Allied landing in Normandy. V.V.

Voroshilov replies that Desmond Tay then gave an account of the events: "Cannons began firing from more than 600 Allied ships.... Thousands of bombers cut the air overhead. Fighters scurry back and forth, appearing and disappearing in clouds of smoke. The Allied attack on Europe begins" [7, c. 322]. A remarkable success of "Reuters" was the report about how Gestapo chief Himmler surrendered to the Allies on April 28, 1945. Also, they were the first to report the discovery of Hitler's body. While in Berlin, Hooper received a message from the Soviets. The American correspondents were headed by air to Paris, and there was no direct train from Berlin. So Hooper asked a British rider to send a dispatch to Lübeck, the nearest point of communication. Four hours later the BBC broadcast this message. The Americans at this time were still in flight. V.V. Voroshilov writes: "The extreme event of the military campaign "Reuters" was the report on August 6, 1944 about the atomic bombing of Hiroshima by the American aviation: "President Truman reported that the first atomic bomb, the most powerful bomb in the world, was dropped 16 hours ago on Hiroshima (west of Kobe), on the Japanese military base by an American army plane. This bomb is more powerful than 20 thousand tons of TNT and has an explosive force 2 thousand times greater than the most powerful bomb used by British aviation during World War II"" [7, c. 323]. Two days later, a Reuters correspondent from Guam transmitted the first interview with the pilot who dropped the atomic bomb.

Consolidating Reuters' status as a global news agency

In the post-war years, the agency began to look for new opportunities to maintain its own influence in the UK, as well as to remain leading globally. In March 1947, the Autralien Associated Press and the New-Zealand Press Association became co-owned by Reuters. At this time, Reuters was attempting to expand its network of correspondents around the globe. After the collapse of the British Empire, it capitalizes on its established economic and information ties to become a global news agency.

An exclusive interview with the first Everest patrons in 1953 brought the agency immense popularity and reader attention. The Times was the first to report the event because climbers Hillary and Tansing were contractually bound to it. However, Peter Jackson, Reuters correspondent in Karachi, organized his own expedition and, after climbing to an altitude of 5,400 kilometers, interviewed the pioneers on the Kumbu massif. After that he sent his assistant to Kathmandu. This is how the world learned about the mountaineers' first impressions.

In reporting on space conquests, the agency benefited from a well-established system of monitoring television and radio messages. M. Magront notes that "on April 12, 1961, Reuters was two minutes ahead of other Western companies in reporting on the flight of Yuri Gagarin into space" [22, p. 74]. [22, c. 74]. The transmission of the first flight to the Moon from the space center in Houston was one minute earlier than that of the American news agency "Associated Press".

Since opening a bureau in eastern Germany, Reuters has been in contact with the All-German News Service. Thanks to this, the agency was the first to broadcast information about the erection of the Berlin Wall in 1961 and then its destruction in 1989. V.V. Egorov writes: "The report of this through the eyes of correspondent Martin Nethersky looked as follows: "Hundreds of East Berliners stand at the site of the wall that has just collapsed, not yet believing what has happened. A group of jubilant FRG citizens staged a spontaneous rally, with participants chanting, "The wall has collapsed! The wall has come down!" Girls are calling their mothers to tell them that they will return home after they go shopping in West German stores" [12, p. 126] [12, c. 126].

In 1963, the general manager of Reuters gave the go-ahead for an aggressive and truly international operation of the agency that would generate wide profits. To this end, a policy of brutal work scheduling was introduced. The management realized that for a technical breakthrough, it was necessary to master computer technology and the transmission of messages through this mechanism. A decision was made to subscribe to the services of Stockmaster, a computer product of Ultronic Systems Corporation. By this time, Reuters was using 22 transatlantic channels. The corporation's engineers, after signing the contract in 1964, developed an amplification system that increased the amount of information transmitted from Stockmaster's main computer across the Atlantic Ocean. Thus, 44 channels began to be used to transmit messages. In addition, the agency received the rights to Stockmaster's exclusive representation in Europe for 10 years.

In 1970, the Videomaster system was introduced. Subscribers were able to receive news about events related to the economy. Through agreements and the use of information technology, Reuters made a profit of about 4 million pounds. The next significant step in introducing computer innovations for the supply of economic information was the creation of the Reuters Man Monitor service. The concept was that the Monitor would display on the screen up to 170 words or 110 letters at a time from a database. This information would be able to be fed for 24 hours in real time. Using microfilm technology, Reuters has created a super-fast, easy-to-use system based on a broad information base. Prior to this, the business community relied on telephone and telex services. "The Monitor" allowed market traders to dial in stock bets and watch competitors on a video screen. Also, information was provided on metals, raw materials, and supply and demand were analyzed.

It is worth noting that discoveries in information technology were constantly being developed. Soon, a computerized messaging system was created to process messages and transmit news around the world as quickly as possible. In 1973, journalists began using television to create and transmit news. "Reuters acquired control of the international television news agency, Wiznews Ltd." The work of technology was supported by the superior skill of correspondents, which implied accuracy and timeliness of information. One of the main distinctions of the agency as a closed joint stock company was the existence of trust income between shareholders.

By 1981, Reuters' financial position was more stable compared to earlier periods. However, managing director Glen Renfrew still urged staff to look for opportunities to make "substantially greater profits". The Board began discussing the possibility of a million pound loan to pay for the operation of Monitor. As A.G. Kiselev notes: "The company was not able to pay for the work with its own resources" [15, c. 16]. There were also opinions that in order to maintain the leading positions in the technological race, in the coming years it will require funds that cannot be obtained through internal turnover.

Naturally, the company's management was looking for an answer to the question: How could such a low-profit organization earn such sums? After all, the news agency could not rely on the traditional sources of income for other media - advertising and sponsorship. That's why the idea came up that the only way to earn significant money was to transform the company into a public joint-stock company. The initiator was the then owner of the Financial Times and one of its directors, Alan Haar. Controversy and debate began, both within the agency and among the British public. The reason for the fear was that the change in status would lead to the elimination of the trust deed, which guaranteed the preservation of the agency's main objectives and independence. However, there were those who favored a change in economic status. A member of the trust, Lord Matthews, in conversations with journalists, outlined the agency's bright prospects in the event of a change of status. He argued that the sale of shares could be started now. If the proposed idea were realized, Reuters would become the world's first news agency - an open information society. Such a thing was a novelty for world communities. By this time, there were only four forms of ownership: state-owned, press cooperatives, closed joint-stock companies and private.

Apart from philosophical disputes about Britain's national patrimony as a news agency, there were technical difficulties. It was unclear how one could, without breaking trust points, put Reuters shares up for public sale. In addition, the ownership patterns of many newspapers had changed slightly since 1941, with some ceasing to exist and others taking their place. Y.S. Voskoboynikov points out that according to the words of the chairman of the Association of Newspaper Owners, Lord Marsh, all this resembled "a stable where there was a dispute about the ownership of shares" [8, p. 137] [8, c. 137]. In addition, there are no proper documents of transfer of shares during the sale or collapse of various newspapers.

Lawyers from the Association of Newspaper Owners spent several weeks in the archives to establish links in the transfer of shares. The owners started accusing each other of molestation. A war of words began. According to Y.S. Voskoboynikov, the chairman of the group "Mail" Lord Hartwell said: "I would rather mortgage my house than allow the world information agency to lose its integrity and independence" [8, p. 138]. [8, c. 138]. After that, the majority was in favor of bridging the divide and supporting change. It was decided to create an organization like the Star Chamber of the British Parliament to settle all disputes. Obviously, a public sale of shares would take place very soon. However, the form of the agency's transformation remained a stumbling block. Three issues were key: 1) how to ensure that the agency, once the shares were sold on the stock market, remained protected from being taken over by a sole proprietor; 2) how to ensure that the safeguards did not diminish the value of the company and the profits of shareholders; and 3) how to reconcile both objectives with the Trust's principles, which were categorical that the integrity and independence of the agency could not be undermined.

Lord Matthews proposed the following solution: if it was Reuters Financial Services that was the main contributor to the agency's profits, then a separate company could be formed on their basis and the shares could not be issued for public sale. After all, there was no mention of financial services in the trust deed. However, this proposal ignored Reuters News Service. Finally, on September 14, 1983, a decision in principle was made that the shares could be freely sold, but limited by many conditions. The three main provisions of the Warburg appraisal agency stated:

1. "Reuters could be valued at between a billion and one and a half billion pounds and would be attractive to UK and US investors.

2. The tax structure of the new company can be structured in such a way that double taxation can be avoided.

3. The transformation of a company into a public company is compatible with considerations of guaranteeing its independence.

At Murdoch's suggestion, a working group was set up and tasked with looking at four possibilities for transforming the company:

1. Financial restructuring to separate editorial activities.

2. Issuance of shares without voting rights but with the right to play in the market.

3. Issuance of marketable shares with limited voting rights, existing holders retain ownership of thirty percent of the capital.

4. Issuance of marketable shares with limited voting rights, existing owners retain a minimum percentage of capital.

At the first meeting of the working group, Matthew-Murdoch's first proposal was rejected as impracticable. As for the second, it was said that the approach presented would likely significantly limit the number of shares that could be offered for sale and reduce their value. Attention focused on the third and fourth claims. The third formula was intended to preserve as many of the company's existing principles as possible and allowed directors to be appointed according to the number and class of shares. The fourth proposal had in mind the replacement of the existing control structure with a special "master share" to be owned by the members of the trust, and they in turn were given the power to block decisions to take over control of Reuters.

S.S. Raspopova writes: "In the midst of the disputes about the forms of sale on September 21 appeared a memorandum by Renfrew-Nelson, who reminded that "the price of truth is higher than many people can imagine"" [31, c. 41]. British Prime

Minister James Callaghan touched upon the legal aspect of the problem, noting that if the trust deed was discussed in 1941 by the House of Commons, then now this body should express its opinion.

On October 25, a joint committee of the Press Association and the Newspaper Owners Association gave clear form to detailed proposals for the final capital distribution scheme. The following proposals were agreed upon: 1) the structure of the new company could remain simple and be as close as possible to the existing one; 2) the shareholders were to retain as little economic interest as possible for the time being; 3) the shareholders of the Newspaper Owners Association were to hold shares individually, but in accordance with the agreement; 4) no shareholder should hold more than fifteen percent of the capital; and 5) the new Board of Directors would include no more than 15 executives.

The conclusion of the meeting was "The agreed inviolability of trust principles is key". It was decided in principle that the entry to the exchange should be made in the spring of 1984. M.I. Skulenko expresses the opinion that "this term seemed to be the only possible one, because in the fall the largest sale of shares in the history of Great Britain was expected - Thatcher's government intended to sell 51% of the state telephone company British Telecom on the market" [34, p. 84] [34, c. 84]. The result of the meeting was the council's decision to implement the sale of Reuters shares on the stock exchange and present the transformation plan to the members of the Test for their comments. A few days later, the CEO of Reuters launched attacks on those who wished to interfere in the affairs of the government and parliament, starting a conversation about the independence of the government. Despite this, the House of Commons still organized a hearing. Nicholas Soames, Churchill's grandson, expressed doubts about the transformation at Reuters. Mitchell recognized the agency's international role and argued that government intervention was necessary not to protect British interests but to protect the interests of the public around the world. Kenneth Baker, the British minister for information technology, emphasized that the agency is a "national asset" because it runs a successful international company with its headquarters in the UK.

Baker expressed satisfaction that the Board and the Trust are committed to protecting the independence of the agency once it goes on sale.

The final decision on the future structure of the company, supported by the members of the Reuters Trust, was made at a Board of Directors meeting on February 21, 1984. A special company, the Founders Company, was created, which owned the "master share" and was to prevent attempts to take over control of Reuters. The powers of the co-owners of the agency were as follows: if a member of the Trust believed that any group had acquired, or was attempting to acquire or retain control of Reuters, a majority of the Trust could use the rights of the Founders Share Company (Founders' Capital) to enforce the trust principles of the agency. If an attempt is made to alter the protective rights of Founders Share, any two members of the Trust can use the rights of "Founders' Capital" in the holding company to prevent this from happening. "Founders' Shareholders' Capital" held by Founders Share, which is not freely tradable but has a minimal economic interest, is capable of preventing attempts to take control of Reuters. The new structure of the news agency did not allow investors to participate in major decisions about the work.

Reuters Holding Limited was incorporated on April 11, 1984. On the same day, the first meeting of the Board of Directors was held. The first decisions in principle were made on the value and number of shares to be sold. The number of those wishing to become co-owners of Reuters exceeded the expected number by 2.7 times. The price for a block of shares was raised. However, the grandiose success did not happen - the company received less than expected - 53 million pounds. Still, this sum was quite significant to give a new impetus. The fundamental reason for the transformation at Reuters was the increasing dominance of financial, speculative capital, associated with the abolition of the convertible dollar into gold in 1971 by Nixon. One of the most tangible consequences of this was the shift of power from the offices of the corporation's directors to the financial markets. the transformation of the news agency into a stock exchange game reflected the Thatcher government's policy of dramatically liberalizing the British economy. It was at this time that the coal industry, railroads, and communications were privatized in Britain.

Liberalization came to the media sphere - the sale of Reuters was one of the first steps. It was followed by the sale of the Times by Roper Murdoch, who then launched the Sky satellite channel (now called BBC), the partial privatization of the BBC (the Pearson Group owns 25% of the world service, which opened in 1991). It is still worth noting the thoroughness with which such a strategic media outlet as Reuters changed its status. The process of its transformation from a closed joint-stock company to a public one took two and a half years. During this time, lines of defense were put in place, most of which were later removed - the onslaught of capital proved too strong. The transformation of Reuters underlined the commercialization of British and world journalism. G. Viren notes that "since 1984 the agency more often began to place economic and financial news" [6, p. 96]. [6, c. 96]. It reoriented to financial products that had nothing to do with journalism. Thus, the transformation of Reuters became an illustration of another monopolistic redistribution of information flows in communication channels. The trade sector needed automated operational services.

According to S.I. Smetanina, "after the transformation in a short period of time the company had about 300,000 shareholders around the world" [35, c. 284]. There were still questions about the possible influence on the work of the agency. Management emphasized that journalistic services are assets of the company, both financially and strategically. First, general news is important for economic services. Second, economic services operate very successfully. Third, the availability of community news that is filed and edited, including the needs of economic services subscribers. The budget and plan for 1985-87 set two major goals for the company: 1) to keep the level of short- and medium-term revenues and profits in line with shareholder expectations; and 2) to ensure the company's future prospects by "aggressive development."

During the 1980s, profit growth was at 30-40%. This indicates that the agency achieved a steady increase in profits. S.I. Smetanina writes: "Aggressive behavior manifested itself in the purchase of "Rich Inc. of Chicago" in 1985 for 58.5 million dollars, as well as the computerized trading system "Instinet" for 100 million dollars in 1987" [35, c.

296]. Henceforth, the agency was perceived by stakeholders as a direct tool for doing business. The pursuit of profits led to all new changes. The economic activities of the agency expanded rapidly. In 1987, new economic products emerge: Equities 2000, Commodities 2000 and Energy 2000. During this period, business and business-to-business news attracted increasing attention from Reuters. in 1989, a sociological study conducted by the agency showed that the world's top ten newspapers took 58 percent of economic news from Reuters, 21 percent from the Associated Press and 11 percent from AFP. The share of economic news in the company's reports amounted to almost 50%.

By the late 1980s, about 2/3 of UK journalists specialized in commercial information. The same news could be presented as both economic and general news. In the 1990s, Reuters develops into one of the world's largest providers of economic services. The agency approves a new holding company, Reuters Group plc. This was explained by the need to take into account the interests of investors in terms of dividends, i.e. profits. Firstly, the holding company makes it possible to immediately return capital to shareholders without significant tax losses. Secondly, it allows reducing the number of issued shares. Thirdly, it makes it possible to pay out surplus capital to shareholders and undertake share repurchases without restrictions imposed by UK law on the reserves intended for distribution.

Thus, the transformation in the economic status of Reuters led to a significant strengthening of economic services over journalistic ones. during this time, 20 new economic products of the company appeared, the agency turned into the largest provider of financial services, most of which have a very distant relation to journalism. It is worth noting that Reuters tried not to work with small consumer firms, but to supply news for global macroeconomic financial institutions.

Since the beginning of the 21st century, Reuters has been referred to as a publicly traded company. As of June 2003, the company had 32431 shareholders, with a total of 1394,000 shares in circulation. The largest shareholders are: investment funds and trusts (32%); pension funds (26%); American depositary shareholders (12%); foreign banks (6%); insurance companies (5%); individual shareholders (4%); corporate holding companies (2%); non-profit organizations (2%); and foreign governments (1%). Other organizations with less than 100,000 shares collectively hold about 10% of the shares. Geographically, the distribution of shareholders is as follows: UK (46%), US (38%), Europe (10%), Asia Pacific (1%), other countries (2%). From this we can see that Reuters is a classic transnational corporation in which Anglo-American shareholders play a key role. Moreover, this is a real cross-border mechanism, which actually made the status of the British agency nominal.

The main governing body of the company is the shareholders' meeting. The meetings are held annually. They consider issues that relate to the most important problems, the company's development plan, including the election of the Board of Directors. It is this authority that manages the company. It consists of 5 executive directors, including the CEO (currently Tom Glocer) and 8 ordinary directors, including the Chairman (currently Christopher Hogg). The Board is elected 6 times a year and also holds a special meeting each year to set the strategy for the coming year. The Board decides on the company's strategy in line with its goals and objectives. It also decides on the budget, major transactions and shareholder capital.

To preserve the traditions of Reuters, a special company of the founders, the Fuanders Company, the Reuters Trust, which consists of 15 people, acts. It is empowered to block evil decisions aimed at changing the status of the news agency or violating its traditions in collecting and disseminating information. The agency has a staff of about 14,000. This is the highest number among all news agencies. However, the number of journalists includes only 2,200. Foreign bureaus account for 197 of them.

Reuters' *financial* products, which contribute to the agency's top earnings, are distributed to 521,000 users in 52,800 locations. These products are divided into financial-information products (customers are supplied with information from financial markets) and operational products (allowing customers to conduct market transactions themselves). Financial-information products are united in the system "3000", which was created in 1997. A.G. Kiselev notes: "These include the following services: "Markets-3000", "Money-3000", Securitis-3000", "Real Estate-3000", "Terjuri-3000" and "3000- Extra"'"" [15, c. 346].

1. "Markets 3000" is a service that covers money, commodity and financial income markets. It delivers real-time market data, news and television, historical information. Powerful computer software allows clients to quickly and easily display, analyze and tailor information to their systems. "Markets-3000" do not have to choose from numerous sources to get a complete picture of the world, what is happening in the market, because the service analyzes and places statistical accounts and more favorable directions. Users are given the opportunity to work faster and do their business.

2. The Money 3000 service is designed for those who work in global money markets. It allows you to make calculations, search for market opportunities, use historical overviews and make economic forecasts. Money and currency traders use it to obtain money rates and relationships, as well as a picture of the money markets. The service gathers information from thousands of different sources to put the compiled information on the client's display, providing them with a complete picture of what is happening in the money markets. This makes it much easier for clients to make decisions, allowing them to act quickly and with confidence.

3. "Securities-3000" allows clients to receive information on securities, indices and macroeconomic data and analyze their condition. Thanks to an extensive database, managers are given the opportunity to select companies for investment according to the necessary criteria.

4. The Real Estate-3000 service is engaged in analyzing the state of real estate markets, current and projected investments in this sphere. The system includes dealing and trading services that allow real-time transactions for clients.

5. The Trejuri-3000 service includes a combination of real-time data, news, a broad database that consists of stock information and historical stock price data. it also offers tools for analyzing stock situations. By utilizing historical information and current Trejuri 3000 market news, brokers can provide clients with in-depth market analysis that adds value to their advice. Real-time financial news, delivered in both text and

television reports, helps traders make their decisions faster.

6. The 3000-Extra system provides combined analytical information on all Reuters financial information products. It provides combined analytical information on all Reuters financial information products.

7. "Open Systems allows consumers to create their own access to financial market data. The client has the ability to combine information from various sources. For example, Reuters information, information from other market sellers and their own. "Open systems" include the Triarch system, which enables clients to receive, distribute and display messages from a variety of sources, the Reuters CCL system, which provides open interface access to real-time information, and the Cobra system, which allows clients to create their own customized editorial equipment.

8. The Euromarket service provides customers with information on trading and investment opportunities. It provides information on prices and quotes from European markets - money, currency, stock and government bond markets.

9. "Reuters Television is part of the Reuters 3000 series of products and is included with no additional subscription price. It provides live coverage of all major economic events in global markets. Reports on contracts, inflation, corporate status and management changes are accompanied by commentary from experts, politicians and anyone else whose opinion may be relevant. Television utilizes Reuters' network of correspondents, as well as the agency's cameras located around the world, including in government and financial institutions.

10. In 2001, Reuters bought the American Internet system Bridge Channel, which requires an ordinary Java program without additional hardware to function. thus, the system provides quotes online.

11. The DataScope service provides messages on historical and reference topics. In addition, the system offers stock information on 180 world exchanges at the end of each day, 175 currency quotes, cross and forward quotes, futures and opportunities.

Reuters' *operational* products are integrated into the global 2000-2 service, which is now a global electronic brokerage system. it provides access to standardized dealer video terminals for customers at financial institutions around the world. The central control center for the system is in London. It is duplicated by branches in Hong Kong, New York, Nicosia and Tokyo. A.G. Kiselev notes that "Reuters' operational products include Dilling-2000-1, Dilling-2000-2, Dilling-2000-2 forwards, Trading Room and Diltracker" [15, p. 358] [15, c. 358].

1. "Dealing 2000-1 is the world's leading service for enabling dealers to communicate with each other. It provides currency and money market traders with the ability to contact and trade with 24,000 trading partners. Traders can select a trading partner across the globe at the touch of a button, and when they receive a response, they can enter into electronic negotiations. Each dealing station can enable simultaneous negotiations with four different partners. At the same time, communication is recorded on special cards, which allows clients to return to the details of the conversation.

2. The Dealing-2000-2 service is an anonymous electronic trading system. It offers quotes on a multitude of currency pairs and allows customers to save significant amounts of money, as consumers do not incur transaction costs.

3. The Dealing-2000-2 Forwards service operates in 21 countries and utilizes 16 forward instruments, offering trades for terms of up to one year, including all intermediate periods.

4. "Trading Room" provides the ability to trade based on real-time market price information. It also allows market participants to advertise stock prices to their clients, who can respond to them and provide guidance through Reuters' reliable, high-speed network. Trading Room's strategic focus is the fixed income market, with government bonds and corporate equities as its focus.

5. The Diltracker system adds value to dealing programs by allowing banks to store information and display data graphically. Electronic dealing systems are a valuable source of information, from trading prices to partner information.

Reuters *news* services include: "World Service", "Business Report" and "Online" services.

1. The flagship of this category is World Service. It caters to media clients. The World Service produces about 600 stories a day, with regularly changing 24-hour coverage ranging from political, diplomatic and social issues to science, business, sports and cultural news. The service analyzes news and makes forecasts in the economic and financial spheres.

2. The Business Report service includes business, economic and financial news, analysis, commentary and forecasts delivered by Reuters' regional services. Information for Business Report is provided by the news agency's four services, which are as follows

operate on different continents: European, North American, Latin American and Asian.

3. Within the Online service, the top 10 news stories are changed hourly in the form of a sammarie and one paragraph. In addition, breaking news stories are added as soon as the events to which they relate occur. News in digest form can be viewed by the audience in a fuller form, including broad context and analysis.

Thus, we can conclude that, firstly, the collection and transmission of information messages in the middle of XIX became very relevant, because by this time society needed coverage of events and phenomena. Also, the development of technology required their promotion in the market of goods. The development of education and capital accumulation created a market for advertisers.

Second, the increase in readership and circulation of London publications entailed the professionalization and industrialization of the press. Reuther's audience was mainly middle-class men of liberal views, so the information the agency published was aimed at them. Liberal-minded Victorians valued accuracy in the presentation of messages, so Reuter's kept a close eye on the quality of its output. By the outbreak of World War I, Reuters had become an agency of the British Empire. This put it out of competition in the domestic market and very much strengthened its position in the international market. Monopolies in the media became a common phenomenon.

Third, the economic changes at Reuters reflected a general trend in the development of news agencies in the early twentieth century. At this time, press associations were being formed to reduce costs in news gathering. After all, news agencies were becoming more and more expensive as technology advanced. In addition to Reuters, companies in Spain, Denmark, and Norway were corporatized. In the states where they were just emerging, the form of press associations on a cooperative basis was maintained.

Fourth, in the post-war years, Reuters found new ways to retain its leading positions in the world information market and to win new ones. The successes of correspondents in journalistic work, as well as competent management policy allowed the agency in the 70-80s of the XX century to firmly establish itself as a world news agency. Also, much attention was paid to economic and financial news. Dealing and brokerage services became an integral part of the financial system. The development of economic activities contributed to the development of Reuters as a business enterprise. It endeavors to supply news for global macroeconomic financial institutions. It is this type of news that began to attract the attention of the company's management.

Fifth, Reuters is a classic transnational corporation, with Anglo-American shareholders playing a key role. In 2008, the agency was bought by Canada's Thomson Corporation, the world's largest media holding company. After the transaction, Reuters and Thomson merged into Thomson Reuters Corporation, which has about 14,000 employees working in 91 countries. The agency is a world leader in the provision of information, so the main priorities in the development of the company are defined as its expansion and investment in information projects. This development strategy allows Reuters to maintain its status in the global market, and the information supplied is in demand among consumers.

The polyvariability of Reuters' creative methods: politics

In the era of competition for the speed of information transmission, journalists have come to value the ability to quickly obtain the necessary information and quickly process it for placement on the pages of the publication. It should be pointed out that the problem of speed, or pace, has influenced the selection of appropriate genres. The role of a news agency is to find fresh information on topics of public interest and to be able to convey it quickly and accurately to its readers. The most important facts that define news are the following: frequency of repetition, magnitude, clarity, sensationalism, and dynamism (development of an earlier event). Among the main requirements that a news report must meet are: promptness, brevity, compactness and accuracy.

1. "Reuters."

Written by Amanda Becker and David Morgan with contributions from Richard Cowan, Doina Kiaku, and Susan Heavey, dated October 20, 2017.

Title: "U.S. Senate approves key budget blueprint for Trump's tax reform".

Lid: "U.S. President Donald Trump's proposed tax reform passed a meaningful hurdle on Thursday after the Senate approved a 2018 budget blueprint that could allow Republicans to pass a tax cut bill without the support of Democrats"" [2].

By. U.S. President Donald Trump. What? Tax reform has passed a meaningful barrier. Where? USA, America. When. Thursday. Why. After the Senate approved the 2018 budget bill. How. Republicans will pass a tax cut bill without Democratic support.

Based on this lede, the reader can familiarize themselves with the information and then get additional information and details: "The Republican-controlled Senate approved the budget bill by a vote of 51 to 49. Its implementation would increase the state budget deficit by $1.5 trillion over the next ten years because of the need to offset proposed tax cuts." The facts allow the material to be more constructive and accurate, with less recourse to emotional coloring. The piece introduces a direct quote from Senate Majority Leader Mitch McConnell: "With this budget, we are on our way to much-needed relief for Americans, for families bearing the burden of an unfair tax code." The author explains the gist of what is happening: "The budget bill passed by the Senate contains a legislative tool that will allow Republicans to approve tax reform with a simple majority vote." The introduction of the words of official sources into the text makes the material factual and accurate: "The White House says the Republicans' plan to cut the corporate income tax rate to 20 percent from 35 percent would create new jobs and raise wages for workers in industry." In this way, the author summarizes the material and provides different points of view.

2. "Reuters."

Written by Isla Binney, dated October 21, 2017.

The title is "Spain to remove Catalonia government from power, hold elections".

LEAD: "Spanish authorities announced Saturday that they would dissolve the Catalan government and hold new elections, citing the goal of the unprecedented move as preventing the region's secession." [5].

By whom? The Spanish authorities. What? Announced the dissolution of the Catalan government and new elections. When? Saturday. Where? In Spain. Why? For the unprecedented step of preventing the secession of the region. Thus it can be seen that the lead answers key questions that help the reader to get into the essence of the event.

Then the author reveals what is happening in Spain: "The plan, which requires approval by Spain's upper house of parliament, the Senate, is designed to resolve the country's most serious political crisis in 40 years, but is unlikely to please the supporters of Catalan independence, who on Saturday plan to take to the streets with protests". A direct quote from Spanish Prime Minister Mariano Rajoy is inserted, "We will ask the Senate, in order to protect the common interests of the people, to approve the government to dismiss the Catalan president and his government." The historical data goes on to say: "This is the first time in Spanish history since the return to democracy in the late 1970s that the central government has exercised its constitutional right to take control of the region and run it directly from Madrid." The journalist explains the plan to readers: "This means that the central government will have full control over the region's police, finances and media. The powers of the regional parliament will also be limited." Structuring the news allows the audience to absorb events more quickly and to stay informed about the political situation without spending a lot of time.

3. "Reuters."

Written by Sam Edwards in Barcelona, Julien Toyer.

Title - "Spain imposes direct rule over Catalonia after independence, dated October 27, 2017.

LEAD: "Spain's upper house of parliament has empowered the government of Prime Minister Mariano Rajoy to govern Catalonia directly, minutes after the region's parliament declared independence." [47].

Who? Prime Minister Mariano Rajoy. What? The upper house of the Spanish parliament has given the right to govern Catalonia directly. Where? In Spain. When? Minutes after the region's parliament declared independence.

The lead is concise, because after reading it, one can immediately understand the essence of the news. The main part starts with the upcoming affairs of Spanish Prime Minister Mariano Rajoy: "Rajoy is expected to convene a cabinet meeting to agree on the first measures to govern Catalonia. These measures could include the dissolution of the government in Barcelovna and the imposition of direct control over the Catalan police." It goes on to say how the political situation is viewed by the country and the international community, "Although the declaration was only a symbolic gesture, since neither Spain nor the international community recognizes the independence of the region, the actions of Madrid and Barcelona have already provoked the worst political crisis in the country in the last forty years." Spanish Prime Minister Mariano Rajoy called for calm, tweeting minutes after the Catalan parliament vote, "I ask all Spaniards for calm. The rule of law will restore law and order in Catalonia." The journalist draws readers' attention to the official documents: "The document approved by the regional parliament in Barcelona, which was boycotted by the opposition, states that Catalonia is an independent, sovereign social-democratic state. The document calls on other countries and institutions to recognize the country's independence." The text also says that Catalonia wants to enter into negotiations with Madrid to establish a new republic. Also, information about the results of the election campaign is given: "70 out of 135 members of the Catalan parliament voted in favor of independence, 10 were against and two abstained, said the speaker of the parliament. Representatives of the Socialist Party, the Popular Party and the Citizens Party left parliament before the vote in protest." Mariano Rajoy is quoted as saying when addressing the Senate: 'It is worth resorting to exceptional measures only when all other measures have been exhausted. It seems to me that there is no alternative. The only thing that can be done and must be done is the adoption and enforcement of the law." This material is not based solely on personal belief and opinion. Direct quotation allows to reflect the views of officials.

4. "Reuters."

The author is Irem Kodja.

Title: "Turkey has purchased S-400 missile systems from Russia - Minister," dated November 13, 2017.

LEAD: "Turkey has completed the purchase of Russian S-400 missile systems, but Ankara is discussing a deal with a European consortium to get help in developing its own missile defense system, Turkish Defense Minister Nurettin Canikli said."[16].

Lid contains a direct quotation of the words of the Turkish Defense Minister. This indicates the reliability of the information. The main part of the piece begins with the opinion of Western allies, who saw the decision of NATO-member Turkey to purchase S-400 systems from Russia as a protest against the alliance. The deal also provoked fears that the S-400 could not be integrated into the NATO weapons system. The journalist goes on to quote a competent person as saying, "A senior NATO commander, Gianikli, told Reuters last week that the alliance would continue to pressure Ankara to buy weapons that can be integrated into NATO systems and that so far Turkey has not received the S-400." The author writes that "sources in the Turkish Defense Ministry said last week that Canikli on Wednesday concluded a letter of intent with France and

Italy to strengthen cooperation in defense projects, including missile defense." Thus, the news item is based on the opinion of a high-ranking NATO commander, indicating that the source of the information is official.

5. "Reuters."

The author is Silvio Castellanos.

The title is "Protesters in Catalonia block roads," from November 8, 2017.

LEAD: "Catalan independence supporters protesting the imprisonment of ousted regional politicians have blocked roads, triggering huge traffic jams at the entrance to Barcelona, and some public transportation routes have almost stopped operating"" [13].

Who? Catalan independence supporters. What? Roadblocks. How? By protesting the imprisonment of ousted regional politicians.

Through the laconic face, the reader can immediately grasp the essence of what is being described, which is evident in this material. Huge traffic jams were caused by several dozen people blocking the region's main thoroughfares, holding placards and chanting "freedom for political prisoners", while social media reported minor clashes as the police attempted to push back the protesters, as evidenced by video footage. The author points to the aftermath of the events that affected Catalonia: "Catalonia's quest for independence has led Spain into its worst political crisis in decades, exacerbating political and cultural divisions and forcing thousands of companies to relocate offices from the troubled region."

The polyvariability of Reuters' creative methods: economics

Every news story has a theme and is preceded by a specific event. The event includes three other elements: source, awareness and time. Moreover, the value of information depends on the source.

1. "Reuters."

Author Charlotte Greenfield.

The title is "New Zealand Prime Minister says ban on foreigners buying homes from early 2018", dated October 31, 2017.

LEAD: "New Zealand Prime Minister Jacinda Ardern said on Tuesday that a ban on foreigners buying real estate will begin in early 2018, but the restrictions will not apply to Australians" [9]. An accurately worded lead includes answers to questions that readers may be interested in.

Who? New Zealand Prime Minister Jacinda Ardern. What? He's announced a ban on buying real estate. Where? New Zealand. When. From the beginning of 2018.

The author goes on to reveal the causal factors that led to this decision: "The housing crisis was left unresolved by the previous National Administration. The politically sensitive housing crisis has shown that prices have risen by more than 50 percent nationally over the past decade. In the city of Auckland, prices nearly doubled during this period. The central bank sees skyrocketing prices as a major economic risk." Then you can find out why exactly Australians are not subject to the ban: "The ban does not apply to Australians because New Zealanders are exempt from restrictions on owning property in neighboring Australia, where many New Zealanders live." Also, factual information is reported, sourced from documents. Some government figures show that the number of home sales including foreigners is only about 3 percent, although Labor has criticized the data and says it excludes many owners, including those who purchase properties through trusts.

2. "Reuters."

The author is Mariki Kochiashvili.

The title is "Bloodhound car launches," dated October 26, 2017.

Leed: "The supersonic Bloodhound vehicle, effectively a fighter jet on wheels, began operations Thursday, eventually reaching 1,000 mph (1,610 km/h)." [18]. At the very beginning of the material, the author places information with accurate data.

The what? The supersonic Bloodhound vehicle. What? It's operational. When. October 26, 2017. Where? In England. How. By reaching 1,000 miles per hour.

The main part of the piece begins with a description of the car: "In front of a crowd of spectators, a blue and orange spaceship with a high tail and long rocket-shaped nose launched two test runs on a 1.7-kilometer (2.7 km) track reaching 200 mph (320 km/h) in about nine seconds". Also, the exact parameters of the car are stated, "It was the first public test of the car, powered by the EJ200 jet engine from the Eurofighter Typhoon, in anticipation of a world record in South Africa in the next few years." The journalist goes on to include a comment from pilot Andy Green: "We came here to say that Bloodhound is coming! And that is exactly what we have been able to demonstrate today. Performance, handling, stability - I can't fault the car at all, it just worked brilliantly". In the final section, the author introduces readers to the project that served to realize this technique. Project Bloodhound was launched in 2008 in London to develop a car capable of reaching speeds of 1,000 miles per hour. About 30 million pounds ($39.49 million) was invested in the project thanks to support from the public and sponsors, including China's Heli Auto Group and Rolls Royce, among others. Also, an assumption is introduced, "If the roughly 13-meter (39ft) long car reaches its 1,000mph target, it will surpass the low altitude record for airplanes of 994mph." For more insight, the reporter compared the car's speed to visual things. For example, at 1,000 miles per hour, it would cover a distance equivalent to more than four soccer fields every second.

3. "Reuters."

Author Elizabeth O'Leary.

Title - Diamond Merlin to open $350 million Legoland in New York State, dated October 26, 2017.

LEAD: "Legoland's third North American theme park, featuring distinctive colorful toys, will be built in New York state for a $350 million investment by Britain's Merlin Intertaimont, the company said in a statement on Thursday." [26]. The lead includes accurate data and answers the main questions:

Who? Merlin. What? Theme park. Where? New York. When? Soon. How? With the company's investment.

The main section begins with the park's geographic location, "The park, dedicated to children's favorite toys, will be built in Goshen, Orange County, 60 miles northwest of New York City, and will serve an area of 23 million people." A comment from the head of the company is further posted: "Merlin, which operates attractions such as Madame Tussauds Wax Museum in London, said the new Legodend is scheduled to open in 2020 and will welcome customers between April and November." The social significance of the park is imagined. After all, its construction provides for more than just an entertainment function. The new facility will create more jobs to combat unemployment, "The park, which will join Legoland parks in California and Florida, is expected to create more than 1,000 jobs, as well as 800 construction jobs as it is developed."

4. "Reuters."

Author Julie Segreti.

The title is "Armani plans to hand over fashion firm's stake," dated October 23, 2017.

Leed: "Giorgio Armani's succession plans include transferring part of his elite fashion empire to his own charitable foundation to prevent any takeover or break-up of the group."

The main section introduces readers to Giorgio Armani and his activities, "Last year, the 83-year-old Armani set up a foundation in his name that he said he plans to spend the rest of his life on. With an estimated fortune of about $6 billion, he is still active in what is Italy's second-largest fashion group but has not named a successor." [33]. According to his succession plan, the foundation, which already owns 0.1% of Giorgio Armani's holding, would take a larger stake. The remaining shares will be held by his heirs, who can only sell their holdings to the foundation. The piece concludes with the company's earnings statistics, "After a 5 percent drop in revenue in 2016, Armani said he expects sales to fall by the same amount both this year and next, but to start growing again from 2019. The group's cash position will improve to €1 billion at the end of this year, up from €880 million in 2016."

5. "Reuters."

The author is Gleb Stolyarov.

The title is "Globaltrack wants to double fleet and become market leader in 3-4 years," dated October 20, 2017.

LEAD: "Russian trucking company Globaltrack, which last week announced plans for an IPO in Moscow, expects to become the market leader in the transportation of complete cargoes, doubling its fleet in 3-4 years on the wave of economic recovery" [36].

Who? Russian road transportation company Globaltrack. What? It expects to become the market leader in the transportation of complete cargoes. Where? Moscow. When? After the IPO in Moscow. How? By doubling its fleet in 3-4 years on the wave of economic recovery.

It can be seen that the lid gathers basic information, which will be further expanded in the publication. The main part starts with a direct quotation. The words belong to the main owner and CEO of Globaltrack Alexander Eliseev: "We have a clear strategic vision to become a national champion in the FTL transportation segment in Russia, so we have a goal of doubling our fleet on the horizon of three to four years." Further information about the company and its products follows: "Globaltrack, which owns a fleet of more than 1,000 road trains (1,090 trucks and 1,170 trailers), calls itself the second trucking company in the FTL transportation market by fleet size after Delovye

Liniya and expects to become the market leader soon." Also, the author publishes the statistics of the Intersectoral Expert Council on Road Transportation": "According to the Intersectoral Expert Council on Road Transportation, the share of road freight transport now accounts for two thirds of all cargo transportation in Russia, and in the medium term it is expected to grow by 3.5 percent per year. In 2016, the transportation of all cargo by road reached 5.14 billion tons, according to the Ministry of Transport." This information will help readers understand the demand for investments in this area, as well as learn about the future direction of the firm's development: "The money, which is planned to be raised through the first IPO in this industry, the company expects to spend, among other things, to increase the fleet by 350-450 road trains and its partial renewal. The fleet increase will contribute to revenue growth, and the renewal will have a positive impact on profitability, as maintenance of a young fleet is several times cheaper than an old one, Eliseev said. According to him, it costs 120,000-130,000 rubles to maintain a new truck in the first year, "in the fifth year it is many times more." According to information provided to Globaltrack by Megaresearch, the total fleet of Russian FTL carriers amounted to 135,000 units at the end of 2016." In the above text you can familiarize yourself with the result of the implementation of this project on the global market. Thus, its benefit becomes obvious. The priority path of the direction is traced: "By betting on business growth, Globaltrack counts on the growth of retail chains, online commerce and on opportunities to consolidate the road transportation market, which is now almost entirely occupied by small companies." In addition, the economic recovery allows to count on the growth of tariffs, which will have a positive impact on profits. Genre - interview.

6. "Reuters."

Author Mark Honrahan.

The title is "Sierra Leone to auction multi-million dollar pro-poor diamond", dated October 23, 2017.

Leed: "Sierra Leone hopes to raise millions of dollars for development projects by auctioning a huge diamond, believed to be one of the largest in the world, in December in New York City." [43].

Who? Sierra Leone. What? Hopes to raise millions of dollars for development projects. Where? New York. When? December. How? By auctioning off a huge diamond.

The main part of the piece begins with information about auctions that have been held before. Also, a feature of the new one is emphasized: "This will be the government's second attempt to sell the 709-carat pearl known as the Peace Diamond, after it rejected the highest bid of $7.8 million at an initial auction in Sierra Leone's capital Freetown in May." The pearls will be sold at an initial auction in Sierra Leone's capital, Freetown, in May." It goes on to reveal the purpose of the auction: "More than half of the proceeds from the sale will be used to fund clean water, electricity, education and health projects in Sierra Leone, and especially in the village of Koryardu, in the Kono region of eastern Sierra Leone, where the diamond was discovered." The journalist includes a comment from an official, namely the chairman of the group of companies that will manage the auction, Martin Rapaport: "There is a reason why nature gave these diamonds to the poorest people in the world and made them the richest people in the world. It's Tikun Olam that makes the world a better place." The final section provides information on what the jewels mean to the territory: "Diamonds fueled Sierra Leone's decade-long civil war, ending in 2002, when rebels forced civilians to mine the stones and bought weapons with the proceeds, leading to the term 'blood diamonds.'"

7. "Reuters."

Written by Gus Trompis.

The title is "Lack of butter leaves French croissants half-baked," from October 24, 2017.

Lid: "There is a shortage of butter in France. Some supermarket shelves are empty and croissant prices are rising, creating a headache for the government" [38]. [38].

It goes on to reveal the cause and effect relationship that can be used to find out why there is a butter shortage in France: "The shortage is the result of falling milk production and rising demand for butter around the world, with consumer attitudes towards distribution. Consequently, rising prices and reduced dairy stocks have put a strain on producers and food processors, with some supply stoppages and with increased costs on retailers and consumers. The following is the opinion of Samir Kichou, a bakery owner in Paris: "As the holidays are approaching, with Christmas preparations and especially for the Galette des Rois cake, which needs a lot of butter, unless there is a significant reduction, we will be forced to pass on price increases." From the piece we can learn that the crisis is sweeping the country, "Supermarkets in the capital and other parts of France have left gaps in their butter sections, and some stores are showing signs explaining the shortage of certain brands." The problem is not just affecting shoppers and consumers. As little is sourced from farms, it is their owners who are bearing the brunt of the burden: "Dairy farmers complain that they get little benefit from soaring butter markets, arguing that what they do get is more often than not due to cheaper prices for raw milk and milk powders." Dominique Chargue, president of the French federation of dairy cooperatives, explains it as follows: "The problem is that in the French market, the right signal has not been given to dairy farmers because prices have not been adjusted to the falling supply of dairy products." The government is taking action, "Agriculture Minister Stéphane Travert said retailers and suppliers must agree price adjustments to maintain supply." It is noted that there are signs of adjustment in the dairy market: lower butter prices. However, the effects of the crisis may linger until the peak holiday demand period at the end of the year.

8. "Reuters."

Author Sarah White.

The title is "Too much sun. Hair too dry: Loreal adds Paris to digital beauty startups," dated October 20, 2017.

Lead: ""Loreal, the world's largest cosmetics company, wants to see more cosmetic technology, such as sensor hair brushes that tell you how to care for your hair and skin creams that let you know how much sun you're getting"" [41]. In Lida, the author provides readers with information about new projects that the cosmetics company is planning to implement.

The main part of the piece begins with a promising development direction: "Loreal is making more and more sales online and providing services and items for high-tech consumers, such as a phone app for virtual makeup tests. The French group said it plans to develop more inventions at a start-up site in Paris, where 10 to 12 firms will work on Loreal projects each year." The following is a comment from Loreal chairman and CEO Jean-Paul Agon: "The world of beauty is already very much digitized. This will allow us to go even further than what we do today. After all, the group's budget for all things digital is growing rapidly. Loreal now spends 35 percent of its budget on digital campaigns and has recruited 1,700 people to work in this area." Also, the journalist notes the further developments the company is aiming for: "In addition to looking for new technologies, such as developments in artificial intelligence or voice recognition software, Loreal will also work with start-ups to develop new cosmetic products, whether creams or makeup, the company says."

Polyvariability of Reuters' creative methods: the social sphere

A news item may be of interest if it contains new information, focuses on key facts, explains how the event may affect society and financial markets, and indicates future developments.

1. "Reuters."

Written by Nerius Adomaitis, Tom Miles.

The title is "Anti-nuclear weapons group wins 2017 Nobel Peace Prize," dated October 6, 2017.

LEAD: "A campaign seeking a global ban on nuclear weapons won the Nobel Peace Prize on Friday, honored by a Nobel committee that cited weapons proliferation in North Korea and said the risk is growing from nuclear war." [1].

Who? The campaign. What? Nobel Peace Prize. Where? Switzerland. When. October 6, 2017. Why. Because there is an increasing risk from nuclear war.

The main part of the piece takes readers back to the story: "Supporters characterized the award as a potential breakthrough for a global movement that has fought to ban nuclear weapons since the day the first atomic bomb was dropped on Hiroshima, Japan, in August 1945". Further information about the campaign is provided, "Aiken describes itself as a coalition of grassroots non-governmental groups in more than 100 countries. It began in Australia and was officially launched in Vienna in 2007." In a speech announcing the prize, Norwegian Nobel Committee leader Berit Reiss-Andersen said the risk that nuclear weapons could be used is greater now than it has been for a long time: "Some states are modernizing their nuclear arsenals, and there is a real danger that more countries will try to acquire nuclear weapons, an example of which is North Korea."

2. "Reuters."

Author Miriam Berger.

The title is "Israel aims not to attract underweight models to the fashion industry," dated October 16, 2017.

Lid: "Israeli lawmakers want to tighten a ban on contracting underweight models and promoting weight loss, as it has been revealed that these measures are routinely ignored, even when taken abroad" [4]. The lead contains the information that follows in a broader way. However, it describes the problem: weight loss promotion.

The main body of the piece begins by describing the topic at hand and identifying the point: "The fashion industry's use of thin-waisted models has long been the subject of heated debate around the world. Critics say the practice promotes an unhealthy body image among women, which can contribute to anorexia, and other eating disorders, and concerns about unrealistic measures of perfection." The legislative level in Israel and other countries is further discussed, "Israel in 2012 became the first country to pass a law requiring advertisers to explicitly identify photoshopped photos and prohibit the use of models below a certain body mass index (BMI), a measure that expresses the ratio of weight to height. Other countries, including France, the center of the fashion industry, have since followed Israel's lead. But unlike Israel's 'anti-photoshopping' law, the French legislation, which went into effect this month, imposes fines and prison sentences on those who do not comply." Also, Israeli photographer Adi Barkan is quoted as saying, "The problem with Israeli law is that there is no punishment. Thus, you continue to contract skinny girls and no one will prohibit it." In this regard, the Israeli government has drafted a new bill: 'Models must obtain a medical certificate confirming a normal BMI. Ads presented in Israel must also clearly state whether they used computer editing techniques to airbrush or reduce the figure." In addition, the reporter took a comment from Israeli supermodel Maayan Keret, who revealed that she developed an eating disorder after she "felt a lot of pressure from everyone" to constantly lose weight. Now, having overcome her illness, she is working to promote positive body images.

3. "Reuters."

Author Gavin Jones.

The title is "Italy has recovered a stolen mosaic from Emperor Caligula's ship," October

22, 2017.

Lid: "A floor mosaic from one of Roman Emperor Caligula's lavish private ships, stolen after World War II, is being returned to Italy from the United States, where it was recovered from a private collection." [10]. Leed introduces a case that has historical roots.

The main part describes the mosaic and indicates where it came from: "The marble, serpentine, and porphyry mosaic from the first century AD came from one of Caligula's ceremonial vessels that was discovered at the bottom of Lake Nemi, near Rome, in the 1930s. The artifact, stolen from Rome's Italian ship museum after the war, was seized by the New York County attorney's office from the collection of an Italian woman living in New York after a police investigation." The final section includes information about items that have also been returned to the places from which they were taken earlier, "Among other Roman objects recovered is a vase from the Apulia region dating to about 350 B.C. that found its way to New York's Metropolitan Museum of Art and two amphorae from the 4th or 5th century B.C. The vase was illegally excavated in the 1980s."

4. "Reuters."

Written by Simon Johnson and Justina Pavlak with contributions from Anna Ringström, Niklas Pollard, Johannes Hellström and Daniel Dixon.

The title is "Nobel Prize in Literature awarded to Kazuo Ishiguro," dated October 5, 2017.

LEAD: "Japanese-born British writer Kazuo Ishiguro has won the 2017 Nobel Prize in Literature, the Royal Swedish Academy of Sciences announced Thursday." [11].

Who? Kazuo Ishiguro. What? The Nobel Prize for Literature. Where? Sweden. When. Thursday, October 5, 2017.

After reading this lead, the reader will be interested in information about the essence of the work of the British writer, as well as what it stood out from the rest. Thus, the journalist further writes in detail about the work: "For the novel "The Rest of the Day", which was released in 1989 and formed the basis of the film of the same name, nominated for eight "Oscars", Ishiguro was awarded the Booker Prize. The Swedish Academy said that in "novels of great emotional power," the writer "revealed the abyss behind our illusory sense of connection to the world." It goes on to provide an insight into the prize: "Ishiguro will receive an award of 9 million Swedish kronor ($1.1 million). Last year's winner of the Nobel Prize in Literature was American poet and musician Bob Dylan." In the final part, the author introduces readers to the literary work of the Nobel Prize winner: "The works of Ishiguro, who moved to Britain as a child, often deal with themes such as memory, time and self-deception, the academy said." Also, the opinion of a specialist is given: "According to the permanent secretary of the Swedish Academy Sara Danius, in the work of the writer "combined Jane Austen and Franz Kafka"". The author reminds outstanding people who have also been awarded the prize: "This triumph puts 62-year-old Ishiguro in line with other winners of the world's most prestigious award in the field of literature - Alexander Solzhenitsyn, Doris Lessing and Ernest Hemingway". Of course, information about the origin of the prize is given: "The prize was named in honor of Alfred Nobel, the inventor of dynamite, and was first awarded in 1901 in accordance with his will for achievements in science, literature, and peacemaking". Thus, the material connects a new event with a historical source. The structuring of the message allows you to familiarize yourself with the information occasion in detail and broaden your horizons.

5. "Reuters."

Written by Alexander Meneghini, Sarah Marsh.

Titled "Active wi-fi hotspots demand more internet access," October 23, 2017.

Lid: "At dusk, as the Caribbean heat subsides, parks around Cuba are filled with families video chatting with loved ones living in another country or browsing social media, their faces lit up by phones and tablets" [23].

The main part of the piece begins with a fact: "The introduction of two wi-fi hotspots in Cuban public places two years ago developed an island with the communist regime. It sparked Cubans' interest in better and cheaper Internet access." The following is a comment from residents, "Maribel Sosa, standing alone with her daughter on the corner of a park in Havana, used video chat to connect with her family in the United States. She recalled standing in line all night to use a public phone to talk to her brother for a few minutes after he emigrated to Florida in the 1980s." Also, the reporter points out the prices of the rates: "Given the relative costs of Internet connections, Cubans use it mainly to stay in touch with family and friends. Despite price cuts, the hourly rate of $1.50 is 5 percent of the average monthly government salary of $30." The state telecommunications monopoly promised to connect the entire island and connected several hundred homes in Havana late last year as a pilot project. Havana's government says it has been slow to develop network infrastructure because of high costs due in part to the U.S. trade embargo. Critics say the government is afraid of losing control. Users say the quality of Internet connections should be improved, as well as measures that preserve privacy policies for messages and calls.

6. "Reuters."

Written by Costas Pitas.

The title is "Oxford to become first British city to ban gasoline and diesel cars downtown," October 12, 2017.

Leed: "The university city of Oxford has unveiled a plan to ban gasoline and diesel cars in its downtown area as part of the most radical set of proposals to reduce pollution" [27]. Lid contains a problem and a method for identifying it.

The main part begins by comparing the two projects: "While London is rolling out an 'ultra-low emission zone' that will see most gas-guzzling vehicles pay a daily toll to enter the city center from 2020, Oxford's Green Emissions Zone will ban car traffic in the city center from the same date." You can further find out how the government came to this decision, "Since German automaker Volkswagen conducted emissions tests in 2015, policymakers around the world have unveiled plans to restrict diesel vehicles in order to improve air quality and realize stricter targets." City Councilman John Tanner commented as follows: "Everyone must take a step - national government and local authorities (businesses and residents) - to end this public health emergency." Oxford will also introduce reduced parking fees for electric vehicles. You can also find out how the program will be implemented, "In the first phase of the plan, cabs, cars, light commercial vehicles and buses that are zero emission will be banned from six streets in the city center from 2020, including near the world-renowned Oxford Union debating society. The zone will be gradually expanded to cover more streets and other vehicle types until 2035, when all emitting vehicles, including trucks, will be banned from the center." Also, United Nations Secretary-General Antonio Guterres is quoted as saying, "Now more than ever, we need a world without nuclear weapons." Mikiso Iwasa, an 88-year-old Hiroshima survivor, told Reuters that the prize would help move things forward, "It's wonderful that we have this Nobel movement to win peace. We all need to join forces, think a lot and move forward to turn this momentum into something even greater."

7. "Reuters."

Written by Niklas Pollard and Anna Ringström with contributions from Johannes Hellström.

The title is "Nobel Prize in Economics awarded for contributions to behavioral economics," dated October 9, 2017.

LEAD: "American Richard Thaler has won the 2017 Nobel Prize in Economics for his contributions to the study of behavioral economics, the Royal Swedish Academy of Sciences announced Monday" [29].

Who? American Richard Thaler. What? The 2017 Nobel Prize in economics. Why. For contributions to the study of behavioral economics. When. Monday, October 9, 2017. Where: Stockholm, Sweden. Source - Swedish Academy of Sciences.

The main part of the piece begins with a direct quotation of the academy's statement awarding the economist a prize of 9 million Swedish kronor ($1.1 million): "Overall, Richard Thaler's contributions have bridged the gap between economic and psychological analysis of individual decision-making." Also, the author informs about the importance of the discovery: "His empirical findings and theoretical results were instrumental in creating the new and rapidly expanding field of behavioral economics, which has had a significant impact on many areas of economic research and policy." Further, the journalist goes back to the history of the award's origin: "The Economics Prize, whose official name is the Swedish National Bank's Alfred Nobel Memorial Prize in Economic Sciences, has been awarded since 1968." Economics was not included in the original list of areas noted in the will of the inventor of dynamite, entrepreneur Alfred Nobel." In addition, the journalist informs about such events: "Last week the names of prize winners in medicine, physics, chemistry, literature, as well as the Nobel Peace Prize were announced." Thus, there is a logical sequence of posted information. The main information is placed at the beginning, and then the mediocre information. The material is built on the principle of "inverted pyramid".

8. "Reuters."

Written by Sarah White, dated October 12, 2017.

The title is " Gucci will give up natural fur from 2018".

The title of the story reflects the event that prompted its writing. Also, the news is direct. The lead reads, "Italian brand Gucci will stop using natural fur in its products from 2018, joining a growing number of fashion houses finding themselves in search of alternatives due to pressure from animal advocates and changing consumer tastes" [40]. The lead is brief and concise. It reflects the essence of the material itself.

Then the author tells about the brand itself and its specifics: "Gucci, which is owned by the Paris-based company Kering, has for many years presented expensive fur coats at fashion shows, and in 2015, under the leadership of creative director Alessandro Michele, released loafers and slip-ons with kangaroo fur trim". The average reader will be wondering what will become of the clothing of the popular brand. The journalist answers the question as follows: "However, the brand has now announced that it will join the companies that have given up the use of natural fur and will sell the remaining fur clothing and accessories at a charity auction. The value of some Gucci mink coats exceeds $40,000." The author also uses direct quotation to confirm the information with first-person words: "Gucci's decision will radically change the future of fashion," said Simone Pavesi of the Italian animal welfare organization." In addition, the statistics of companies that take part in such a program are given: "In 2016, the Italian company Giorgio Armani promised to stop using fur, saying that the development of technology makes animal cruelty unjustified, while the American brand Calvin Klein took a similar step back in 1994". This is followed by detailed information about the reasons for the rejection of natural fur: "Opponents of fur use regularly protest at fashion shows around the world, calling for an end to animal cruelty, and luxury buyers - especially the younger generation - are becoming increasingly sensitive to environmental issues. In this way, the material introduces the audience, allowing them to become fully familiar with Gucci's choices.

9. "Reuters."

Author Estelle Shirbon.

The title is "Dove brand at center of scandal again over video", dated October 9, 2017.

Lid: "The media backlash over the Dove soap commercial, where a dark-skinned woman turns into a white woman, turned into a real disaster for the Unilevel brand" [44].

Who? The Dove Company. What? Media coverage. Where? British TV commercial. When? October 2017. Why? Because a dark-skinned woman turns into a white woman. It's racially charged.

Further information is provided about the essence of the commercial and the reason that attracted public attention: "A three-second clip posted on the brand's Facebook page reminded some users of a racist soap ad from the late 19th and early 20th centuries in which dark-skinned characters scrubbed off their skin to become white". The author begins the post by pointing out how Dove acted, "Dove removed the commercial and apologized. However, the apology did not help to contain the flow of criticism on the Internet - some users called for a boycott of Dove products, and the leading media in the U.S. and Europe picked up the high-profile news". Then we can find out what caused the special attention to this commercial: "In the full version of the commercial, a dark-skinned woman takes off her shirt, turning into a white woman, who then also takes off her shirt and turns into an Asian woman." The company's response is also posted: "The short clip was meant to demonstrate that Dove soap is for every woman and celebrate diversity, but we failed to do so." The journalist points out that this is not Dove's first time and reminds readers that: "The last time a Dove ad caused widespread outrage was in 2011. The commercial showed three women standing side by side, accompanied by "before" and "after" pictures of using the company's products. In the "before" picture, the woman was dark-skinned and the "after" picture was white. At the time, the company claimed that all three women in the commercial were supposed to "demonstrate the effect of the product after use".

Having studied the thematic focus of the materials of the Reuters news agency, the following conclusions can be drawn. First, Reuters correspondents work in more than 100 countries around the world, so international political news states events that take place on a vast territory. This coverage allows the agency to be one of the main providers of information, as the availability of an expanded base provides an opportunity to be the first to learn about major events. Also, in the materials, the company often introduces direct quotation of the words of high-ranking officials, which indicates reliable information. It should be taken into account that the journalist does not express his opinion on a political situation, but only states the fact. This method of work allows not to impose the company's point of view on the readers, but provides an opportunity to comprehend the information received. The audience is given the opportunity to develop analytical skills.

Secondly, Reuters is a leading provider of financial information for professional participants of financial markets, so the agency pays special attention to economic topics. The news is based on accurate data and market indicators. The style follows such parameters as structured, concise and meaningful. In addition, the journalist compares indicators and has the opportunity to make assumptions on a given topic. Readers can find out the growth rates of certain goods and make a plan to realize their resources. It should be noted that economic news can influence market conditions, as investors seek to optimize their goods after information about quotes. It is relevant for a news agency to post such information, thus it is possible to attract the attention of the audience, which will periodically visit the site and follow the information.

Third, the selection of facts plays an important role in Reuters' coverage of social issues. The task of revealing and analyzing a social event comes to the fore. Journalists emphasize not only the statements of officials, but also the opinion of citizens. Also, there is background information about companies and events. The authors present and justify the positions of different social groups, create an opportunity to express views and assessments within different situations. The purpose of social journalism is to maintain stability in society, so the reader can familiarize himself with both a news event and get additional information on a given topic. The materials of this topic are aimed at the formation and implementation of social policy.

Conclusion

Information agencies are currently one of the main subjects of media processes, largely determining the content, volume, and thematic orientation of information flows. Researchers believe that the strengthening of the importance of these structures and in the future, the growth of their number and power due to the rapid development of information technologies.

Firstly, the history of the Reuters news agency begins with the activities of Julius Reuter. It was he who in 1850 started a business by selling economic information from the stock exchange in Brussels and Aachen. The transformation of Reuters into a public limited company, the introduction of computer technology and the sale of economic products really brought about a change in the market. The global financial industry became the main reference point. It was the news tradition that allowed Reuters to successfully conquer financial niches. As much trust in the general news of the company increases, so does it increase in the agency's economic products. Having earned a name and image, Reuters is taking full advantage of it in the economic market. With the birth and development of digital technology, satellite communication, the fusion of computer and communication innovations and the emergence of the Internet, Reuters has revised its existing organization and mode of operation, thus maintaining its status as a dynamic media. With the emergence of new communication channels, it has expanded its audience reach, increased the number of clients and subscribers, and created new service opportunities.

Second, we should list the key principles that influence the activities of a news agency: the desire to maximize profits in a competitive environment, requiring the establishment of strong institutional ties with their clients, by creating communities of interest united by exclusive information, innovative technologies and business opportunities. These factors have had a defining influence on economic news agency over the past decades of their history. For example, the terminal "Reuteres Markets Monitor" allows an investor to estimate the value of a block of shares held by him at a certain moment, to see the price dynamics, and with the help of built-in programs to analyze their development patterns, to get additional information about the shares in the form of a database for further analysis, to select news about the company for a certain period, and to get the most operative facts from the stock market.

Third, the standards of a news agency suggest that the news should be prompt, reliable and objective, contain all the information necessary to assess the importance and consequences of the described event, be understandable, and emphasize the main points. Journalists use simple words, explain special terms so that every interested reader can understand the news.

Fourthly, the agency has developed uniform requirements to the material, which guide correspondents. This is especially true for the structure of the texts of news reports, approaches to their preparation and verification, and criteria for their selection from the flow of events. Common to all news reports is their internal structure. Materials of different thematic focus, volume and genres consist of such standard structural components: headline, lead, sablid (other paragraphs), background. This allows readers to trace the chain of events that preceded the given material.

Fifth, the peculiarity of editing of news agency materials is related to the fact that reports come in a continuous stream and need to be published as quickly as possible. It turns out that there is very little time to correct each story. The unified requirements for a story, which must be followed by both the correspondent and the editor, are as follows: each story describes one main news fact,

the structure corresponds to the "inverted pyramid" principle (the main information is written at the beginning of the message), only the information that contributes to the disclosure, explanation, perception of the main news fact should be written. The management of these criteria allows to publish materials faster and increase the potential audience, which entails maintaining a stable financial condition of the company and the possibility to invest funds for investment projects.

Sixth, in political stories, journalists rely on the words of officials. Quotations allow to use many means of enhancing expressiveness and evaluation. As part of quotations, they acquire the qualities of "fact", which removes the responsibility for their use from the agency. Economic information implies logical presentation of information. The search for profits leads agencies to pay more attention to financial information, namely: share values, prices, quotes, financial charts, market analysis, investment potential, indicators of companies and industries. It should be noted that the agency's establishment of an electronic brokerage network, which includes operational products and does not require any intermediaries between the agency and the client, was a significant step towards raising the status of Reuters. The materials of social topics are focused on meaningful information for a wide audience.

Literature

1. *Adomaitis, N.* The group to combat nuclear weapons won the 2017 Nobel Peace Prize / N. Adomaitis // Reuters.com [Electronic resource]. - 2017. - Mode of access:

http://www.reuters.com/article/us-nobel-prize-peace/anti-nuclear-campaign-group-wins-2017-nobel-peace-prize-idUSKBN1CB0XR. - Access date: 06.10.2017.

2. *Becker, A.* The U.S. Senate approved the key for Trump's tax reform draft budget / A. Becker // Reuters. com. [Electronic resource]. - 2017. - Access mode: https://reuters.com/article/topNews. - Date of access: 20.10.2017.

3. *Belova, L.I.* Universal journalism / L.I. Belova. - M., 2016. - 480 c.

4. *Berger, M.* Israel aims not to attract underweight models to the fashion industry / M. Berger // Reuters.com [Electronic resource]. - 2017. - Mode of access: http://www.reuters.com/article/us-israel- fashion/israel-targets-fashion-industry-over-underweight-models-idUSKBN1CL1S6. - Date of access: 16.10.2017.

5. *Binney, I.* Spain will remove the government of Catalonia from power, hold elections / I. Binney // Reuters.com. [Electronic resource]. - 2017. - Access mode: https://reuters.com/article/topNews. - Date of access: 21.10.2017.

6. *Viren, G.* Information agencies: how news is created / G. Viren. - M., 2015. - 176 c.

7. *Voroshilov, V.V.* Journalism / V.V. Voroshilov. - SPb. : Mikhailov V.A. Publishing House, 2002. - 656 c.

8. *Voskoboynikov, Y.S.* Journalist and information. Experience of the Western press / Y.S. Voskoboynikov. - M., 1993. - 208 c.

9. *Greenfield, S.* The Prime Minister of New Zealand announced a ban on foreigners buying housing from the beginning of 2018 / S. Greenfield // Reuters.com [Electronic resource]. - 2017. - Mode of access:

http://www.reuters.com/article/us-newzealand-politics-housing/new-zealand-pmsays-ban-on-foreign-home-buyers-to-start-early-2018-idUSKBN1D00AR. - Date of access: 31.10.2017.

10. *Jones, G.* Italy has returned the stolen mosaic from the ship of Emperor Caligula / G. Jones // Reuters.com [Electronic resource]. - 2017. - https://reuters.com/article/oddlyEnoughNews. - Date of access: 22.10.2017.

11. *Johnson, S.* The Nobel Prize in Literature awarded to Kazuo Ishiguro / S. Johnson // Reuters.com. [Electronic resource]. - 2017. - Access mode: https://reuters.com/article/oddlyEnoughNews. - Date of access: 05.10.2017.

12. *Egorov, V.V.*. On the way to the information society / V.V. Egorov. - M., 2006. - 192 c.

13. *Castellanos, S.* Protesters in Catalonia blocked the roads / S. Castellanos // Reuters.com [Electronic resource]. - 2017. - Access mode: https://ru.reuters.com/article/topNews. - Date of access: 08.10.2017.

14. *Kim, M.N.* Genres of modern journalism / M.N. Kim. - SPb. : Mikhailov V.A. Publishing House, 2004. - 336 c.

15. *Kiselev, A.G.* Theory and practice of mass information / A.G. Kiseleva. - MOSCOW: KNORUS, 2009. - 432 c.

16. *Kodja, I.* Turkey has purchased S-400 missile systems from Russia - Minister / I. Kodja // Reuters.com [Electronic resource]. - 2017. - Access mode: https://reuters.com/article/topNews. - Date of access: 13.10.2017.

17. *Kolesnichenko, A.V.* Preparation of texts / A.V. Kolesnichenko. - Moscow : Yurait Publishing House, 2017. - 292 c.

18. *Kochiashvili, M.* Bloodhound car starts / M. Kochiashvili // Reuters.com [Electronic resource]. - 2017. - Access mode: http://www.reuters.com/article/us-britain-car/bloodhound-car-kicks-off-bid-to-speed- into-record-books-idUSKBN1CV31J. - Date of access: 26.10.2017.

19. *Lazutina, G.V.* Genres of journalistic creativity : textbook for university students

/ G.V. Lazutina, S.S. Raspopova. - Moscow: Aspect Press, 2011. - 320 c.

20. *Lashchuk, O.R.* Editing information messages: textbook for university students / O.R. Lashchuk. - Moscow : Aspect Press, 2004. -159 c.

21. *Lotman, Y.M.* The structure of artistic creativity / Y.M. Lotman. - M., 1970. - 285 c.

22. *Magront, M.* News as a profession / M. Magront. - M., 2015. - 120 c.

23. *Meneghini, A.* Active wi-fi hotspots require more Internet access / A. Meneghini // Reuters.com [Electronic resource]. - 2017. - Access mode: http://www.reuters.com/article/us-cuba-internet/enthused-by-wi-fi-hotspots- cubans-clamor-for-more-internet-access-idUSKBN1CS1V0. - Date of access: 23.10.2017.

24. *Muratov, S.V.* Active methods of discussion in journalism / S.V. Muratov. - M., 1991. - 203 c.

25. *Nakoryakova, K.M.* Literary editing of mass media materials / K.M. Nakoryakova. - M., 1994. - 189 c.

26. *O'Leary, E.* Diamond Merlin to open $350 million Legoland in New York State / E. O'Leary // Reuters.com [Electronic resource]. - 2017. - Mode of access: http://www.reuters.com/article/us-merlin-ent-

legoland/britains-merlin-to-open-350-million-legoland-in-new-york-state-idUSKBN1CV18C. - Date of access: 26.10.2017.

27. *Pitas, K.* Oxford will become the first British city to ban gasoline and diesel cars in the center / K. Pitas // Reuters.com [Electronic resource]. -2017 . - Mode of access:

http://www.reuters.com/article/us-britain-autos-oxford/oxford-to-become-first-uk-city-to-ban-petrol-and-diesel-cars-from-center-idUSKBN1CH1IQ. - Date of access: 12.10.2017.

28. *Pogorely, Yu.A.* Information agency: style of operative messages / Yu.A. Pogorely. - M., 2000. - 36 c.

29. *Pollard, N.* Nobel Prize in Economics awarded for contribution to the development of behavioral economics / N. Pollard // Reuters.com [Electronic resource]. - 2017. - Access mode: https://reuters.com/article/oddlyEnoughNews. - Date of access: 09.10.2017.

30. *Prokhorov, E.P.* The art of publicism / E.P. Prokhorov. - M., 1984. - C. 324.

31. *Raspopova, S.*S. Fundamentals of journalistic activity / S.S. Raspopova. - M., 2017. - 272 c.

32. *Sapunov, V.I.* Foreign information agencies / V.I. Sapunov. - SPb. : Mikhailov V.A. Publishing House, 2006. - 366 c.

33. *Segreti, D.* Armani plans to transfer a share of the fashion firm / D. Segreti // Reuters.com [Electronic resource]. - 2017. - Access mode: http://www.reuters.com/article/us-italy-fashion-armani-succession. - Date of access: 23.10.2017.

34. *Skulenko, M.I.* Persuasive impact of publicism / M.I. Skulenko. - Kiev, 1986. - 175 c.

35. *Smetanina, S. I.* Media text in the system of culture. Dynamic processes in the language and style of journalism of the late XX century / S.I. Smetanina. - M., 2002. - 382 c.

36. *Stolyarov, G.* Globaltrack wants to double its fleet and become the market leader in 3-4 years / G. Stolyarov // Reuters.com [Electronic resource]. - 2017. - Access mode: https://reuters.com/article/oddlyEnoughNews. - Date of access: 20.10.2017.

37. *Tangate, M.* Media giants : how the largest media companies survive in the market and fight for leadership : translation from English / M. Tangate. - M. : Alpina Business Books, 2006. - 251 c.

38. *Trompis, G.* Lack of oil leaves French croissants half-baked / G. Trompis // Reuters.com [Electronic resource]. - 2017. - Access mode: http://www.reuters.com/article/us-france-food-butter. - Date of access: 24.10.2017.

39. *Tumilovich, N.V.* Fundamentals of creative mastery : educational-methodical complex / N.V. Tumilovich. - Minsk : BSU, 2014. - 152 c.

40. *White, S.* "Gucci will refuse natural fur from 2018" / S. White // Reuters.com. [Electronic resource]. - 2017. - Access mode: https://reuters.com/article/oddlyEnoughNews. - Date of access: 12.10.2017.

41. *White, S.* Too much sun. Hair too dry: "Loreal" adds Paris to digital color startups / S. White // Reuters.com [Electronic resource]. -2017 . - Mode of access:

http://www.reuters.com/article/us-loreal-digital/too-much-sun-hair-too-dry-loreal-adds-paris-to-digital-beauty-start-up-cities-idUSKBN1CP1RY. - Date of access: 20.10.2017.

42. *Frolova, T.I.* Information agencies. How news is created / T.I. Frolova. - M., 2005. - 176 c.

43. *Honrahan, M.* Sierra Leone will auction a multi-million dollar diamond for the benefit of the poor / M. Honrahan // Reuters.com [Electronic resource]. - 2017. - Mode of access: http://www.reuters.com/article/us-sierraleone-diamond- israel/sierra-leone-to-auction-multi-million-dollar-diamond-to-benefit-poor- idUSKBN1CS1IB. - Date of access: 23.10.2017.

44. *Shirbon, S.* Dove brand was again at the center of a scandal because of the video / S. Shirbon // Reuters.com [Electronic resource]. - 2017. - Access mode: https://reuters.com/article/oddlyEnoughNews. - Date of access: 09.10.2017.

45. *Shkondin, M.V. The* system of mass media as a factor of public dialog / M.V. Shkondin. - M., 2002. - 120 c.

46. *Shostak, M.I.* News journalism: issues of technology / M.I. Shostak. - M., 1996. - 96 c.

47. *Edwards, L.* Spain introduced direct governance of Catalonia after the declaration of independence / L. Edwards // Reuters.com [Electronic resource]. - 2017. - Access mode: https://reuters.com/article/topNews. - Date of access: 27.10.2017.

More Books!

yes I want morebooks!

Buy your books fast and straightforward online - at one of world's fastest growing online book stores! Environmentally sound due to Print-on-Demand technologies.

Buy your books online at

www.morebooks.shop

Kaufen Sie Ihre Bücher schnell und unkompliziert online – auf einer der am schnellsten wachsenden Buchhandelsplattformen weltweit! Dank Print-On-Demand umwelt- und ressourcenschonend produzi ert.

Bücher schneller online kaufen

www.morebooks.shop

info@omniscriptum.com
www.omniscriptum.com

OMNIScriptum

MIX
Papier aus verantwortungsvollen Quellen
Paper from responsible sources
FSC® C105338

Printed by Books on Demand GmbH, Norderstedt / Germany